Simple Solutions™

Come, Sit, Stay

By
Arden Moore
Illustrations by Buck Jones

IRVINE, CALIFORNIA

The dogs in this book are referred to as *he* and *she* in alternating chapters.

Library of Congress Cataloging-in-Publication Data
Moore, Arden.
Come, sit, stay / by Arden Moore ; illustrations by Buck Jones.
p. cm. — (Simple solutions)
ISBN 1-931993-42-4 (softcover : alk. paper)
1. Dogs—Training. I. Jones, Buck, ill. II. Title. III. Series: Simple solutions (Irvine, Calif.)

SF431.M818 2004
636.7'0887—dc22

2004003346

BowTie Press®
A Division of BowTie, Inc.
3 Burroughs
Irvine, California 92618
Printed and bound in Singapore
10 9 8 7 6 5 4 3 2

Contents

Introduction

If only we could wave a magic wand over every dog on this planet so that, with one swish, canines from all continents would automatically heed these three commands: *come*, *sit*, and *stay*. There are many reasons why these three commands are so doggone vital. First and foremost, they can be lifesavers. Say, for example, you have a dog who's determined to chase a squirrel into the street. If she had learned to heed the *come* command, she would brake her paws, stop, turn around, and return safely to

ABRACADABRA...
COME! SIT! STAY!
POOF

you after hearing you shout "Come!" Also, if your dog learns the *come* command, you'll never again have to coax, beg, or chase your dog home.

Secondly, dog people love to show off their dogs, whether they're at home, in public, or visiting friends. Secretly, they want their well-mannered dogs to earn compliments for good behavior. For their part, dogs unabashedly solicit head pats and treats.

Having a dog who understands these basic commands will do wonders for both of you! For instance, when the doorbell chimes and your dog outraces you to the front

SIT!

door, imagine the praise you both receive when you simply ask your dog to sit and she resists her strong urge to jump on the visitor. Instead, she quickly complies with your command, allowing your guest to enter without being tackled.

Thirdly, when you are consistent with these commands and your dog learns to obey them, there's no longer any confusion as to who truly ranks as "top dog" in your household. Dogs understand and even appreciate hierarchy. They like to know exactly where they fit in the family ranking. And, it doesn't upset them if they realize they are ranked behind you—and even the cat. It's cool with them. A clear pecking order is illustrated when you ask your dog to stay and she obediently stops in her tracks.

Finally, mastering these three commands can act as a springboard for your dog. Since dogs are always eager to learn, they will feel confident about conquering new commands and cool new tricks. Consider the commands *come*, *sit*, and *stay* as laying a foundation for other actions that your dog will perform willingly on cue, whether you hold a tasty treat in your hand, a dog-loving visitor awaits in anticipation, or she simply wants to please you.

Great Secrets for Training Success

It doesn't matter whether you are teaching your dog the basic commands or advanced tricks. Understanding how he thinks and recognizing what motivates him plays a huge role in the mastery of these commands. Here are some crucial tips that can serve as a foundation for training success.

Ahem: attention, please! The only way to get your dog to comply with your training is to have his undivided attention. Dogs get distracted easily, just like children (and some adults, for that matter). So, when you begin any training session, pick a place and a time where distractions are kept to a minimum. When you're ready, say your dog's name, and wait for his eyes to meet yours. Clap your hands

or whistle if you have to, and make sure he is watching you and waiting for his cue to see what to do next.

Be a leader, not a bully. Think back to your school days. Which kind of teacher did you respond to: the one who loaded up on the homework right before a holiday break and ridiculed students in class, or the one who guided the class gently and who took a special, motivating interest in the students? Dogs, to some extent, react to teaching much like human students do. Sure, most obey when orders are barked at them. But as your dog's teacher, you win his unconditional loyalty by being an effective leader who doesn't need to raise her voice or berate her pupil. Remember: positive verbal feedback motives your dog.

Give me a C—for consistency. Decide on what verbal and physical cues you want to use for the commands of *come*, *sit*, and *stay*. And then . . . stick with them! If you use the *stay* command in one training session and then ask your dog not to move in the next, you will create confusion.

Dogs all learn at different rates, just as people do. For example, your dog may pick up your cues on the first day, while your neighbor's dog may take a few days, or even a

week. That's okay. If you are consistent with the commands, your dog will eventually catch on.

Tone of voice counts. When you teach your dog the three basic commands, make sure the tenor of your voice is friendly, engaging, and confident. If you are feeling frustrated or impatient during the training lesson, your dog will pick up those anxious emotions and the lesson will be a failure. Dogs don't need fancy college degrees to deduce our stress levels!

Avoid mindless chatter. Dogs understand simple, imperative sentences—those with a noun (the dog's name) and a verb (the action you desire). They are less successful with complex sentences. During training, you are more apt to get your dog to respond if you simply say "Oliver, sit" rather than "Hey, Oliver, since this is such a great day, why don't we go outside and practice your *sit* command?" To most dogs, the latter sentence could easily mean "Blah, Oliver, blah, blah, blah, blah, blah, blah . . . ."

BLAH, OLIVER, BLAH, BLAH,
BLAH, BLAH, BLAH, BLAH,
BLAH, BLAH, BLAH, BLAH,...
ZZZZZZZZZZZZZZZZZ

Stick with small reward treats. Training time should be fun for your dog, and that's why using treats works so well. However, keep those tasty morsels smaller than your thumbnail—they should be small enough for your dog to bite once and swallow. By using small treats, you keep his attention on you—and that treat bag you're holding—rather than on chewing the treat.

Keep lessons short. Dogs learn better in training segments that are 10 minutes or less (unless you have a truly attentive dog). You'll notice that, after you begin, your dog's attention span starts to wane with each passing minute. Therefore, you should maximize the use of time during the first five minutes. These mini training sessions actually work better for you since they fit easily into your busy schedule. For example, you can squeeze in a short training lesson before you head off to work or when you get home after a long day.

Think Las Vegas, baby! Slot machines, by design, do not deliver a payoff with each grab of the handle. If they did, Las Vegas' famous strip would be a bankrupt ghost town. Gamblers are attracted to slots because of the hope of hitting a jackpot. Psychologists call this intermittent

SHORT LESSON?
SHORT ATTENTION SPAN.

reinforcement. Apply this theory to canine training. Once you've taught your dog the basics, you can bolster compliance by offering a treat intermittently. Keep your dog guessing about when he'll be rewarded and he'll work harder for that tasty jackpot.

Praise the good and ignore the bad. Another subtle but vital training tip is to reinforce good behavior in your dog. As for inappropriate behavior, learn to ignore it or distract your dog so he stops the misdeed (like chewing your leather shoe); then, divert him with an appropriate option (such as his own chew toy instead of your shoe). In time, your dog will learn there are rewards (praise and treats) awaiting him if he does what you ask.

Vary your locale. Your dog may be a picture of perfect obedience inside your living room but act like a canine Dennis the Menace at the dog park. Why? Your dog needs to learn these basic commands in all types of settings. This way, he learns he must obey you no matter where he is. Once you have success

in the confines of your home, gradually reinforce these commands with him in other settings.

Know when training tools are needed. Puppies—and some strong-willed dogs—may want to test you. Don't match might with might or stubbornness with stubbornness. Instead, consider a training tool. For example, a training halter guides your dog's head toward you without the need for force; it also reduces leash yanking. Time-outs—putting your dog in a bathroom or other safe, confined room with a bowl of water (but no toys or treats) for 10 minutes—can effectively stop an unwanted behavior because dogs are pack animals and don't want to be isolated. Your dog will quickly learn which behaviors land him in a time-out room and which ones garner your praise and attention.

Clicker training—the use of a specific sound to signal to your dog that he made the right move—is based on positive reinforcement. Each time your dog does what is expected, he hears a click sound and knows that praise and/or a treat are soon to follow. If you want to use the clicker method to teach any command, you have many sound-making options. You can purchase an inexpensive canine clicker at most pet supply stores, you can click a

CLICK!

ballpoint pen, or you can make a clicking sound with your tongue against the roof of your mouth. The sound of the clicker indicates the end of the requested behavior and lets your dog know it is okay to get up. Timing is essential if you use the clicker method. You cannot wait even a few seconds after clicking to give your dog his reward. It must follow instantaneously.

End positively. Prepare your dog for continued success by concluding a training lesson when your dog performs well. For example, if he sits four times in a row, stop the lesson and move on to something else.

Conquering the Come Command

Some puppies excel at performing fancy tricks in front of a crowd. They can show their belly, perform a figure-eight maneuver between your legs, or retrieve a dropped writing pen. But, if your dog doesn't always return to your side on cue, she needs to learn the *come* command.

You have to learn how to outsmart your puppy. If you are a consistent leader, she will race your way when you tell her to come, even when she is in mid-spring with a

Jack Russell terrier at the local dog park. Don't be dismayed if, initially, your puppy or newly adopted dog struggles with this command. Persist.

Treat the *come* command like magic. Resist the temptation to call your dog only to reprimand her for digging in the garden or chasing your cat. She will quickly associate the word come with a prelude to punishment or, at the very least, a signal that playtime and fun is over. Each time your dog heeds your *come* command, she should be praised so that she associates compliance with positive feedback.

"COME!"
TA-DA!

In teaching the *come* command, set your dog up for success by holding the first few lessons in locations where there are few distractions. As your dog shows proficiency, gradually add distractions on purpose so that you can continue to remain the top attraction in your dog's mind. There are many ways to teach—and reinforce—the *come* command.

One of these ways is called Pass the Puppy. Young puppies, especially, seem to like this way of learning the *come* command. With the aid of three or four other people, sit in a circle in a large room or enclosed outdoor area. Make sure everyone in the group has a handful of small treats. Place your puppy in the middle of this circle of people. You start the game by calling out her name and then asking her to come. Coax the puppy to you by holding a treat in your extended hand. When she scoots over, give her the treat and some praise. Then, have someone else in the circle call your puppy. Again, finish with a treat and praise. Keep your puppy guessing which person is calling for her so that she must pay attention. Eventually, she'll start associating the *come* command with positive payoffs. Limit this game to five minutes or so, but repeat it daily.

Another way to teach the *come* command is called Out on a Line. First, develop a reliable recall by fastening a long clothesline—about 40 feet—to your canine's collar.

Do this when there are not a lot of canines around to distract her. You should be in an enclosed outdoor area, like a fenced backyard or a dog-friendly park. Let her sniff and explore ahead of you and then, in an upbeat tone, say her name followed by the *come* command as you reel her back with the clothesline. Your dog should turn to look at you and then head your way. When she comes to you, gently grab her collar, hand her a treat without bending over, take a few strides side by side, and then say, "Okay, go play!" Then, loosen the line again. This technique encourages your dog to come back to you because she knows she isn't being reprimanded for some dastardly doggy misdeed and party time is not over when she obeys. Never ask her to come to signal the end of your outing. Say another phrase, such as "let's go" so your dog remains responsive to the *come* command.

There are a couple of classic children's games that can be converted into canine versions to help you teach the *come*

command. One is I Hide, You Seek. Using this game is a fun and effective way to teach your dog the *come* command. It's a great way to introduce the *come* command to a puppy or a newly adopted dog who may lack obedience basics. The rules of this game are simple and easy to follow. Practice this game inside your house with the help of a friend or family member. When you begin, instruct someone to hold onto to your puppy or new dog as you dash into another room. Then call your dog's name in a friendly upbeat voice and ask her to come. You may need to repeat her name a few times until she reaches you. When

she does, give her praise and a small food treat. As you are rewarding her, have your friend hide and call out her name and ask her to come. Do this back and forth a few times and then call it quits for the day. This game teaches the *come* command and it also trains her to be persistent in her search for you—both good skills in case the two of you ever get separated accidentally outdoors.

The other classic children's game that has been adapted for dogs is Tag! You're It!. Start the game with your dog on a leash in an enclosed room or fenced backyard. Call out "Tag! You're it!" as you lightly tap your dog on the back and run in the opposite direction. Let the leash trail behind your dog. Then, kneel down and deliver lots of praise when your dog turns and bounds your way or sits

TAG!
YOU'RE IT!

down in front of you. Repeat this a few times until she understands the rules of this game.

Now, remove the leash but stay in a confined area. Repeat the game a few more times. If your dog does not come your way, stop abruptly. With your back to your dog, bend over and pretend to study a blade of grass or some other object with great attentiveness. The idea is to get your dog to stop, come over to you, and see what is calling your attention away from your game of chase. This is an effective game in the event you and your dog are out and she breaks loose and begins running away from you.

Instead of chasing after her, simply yell "Tag! You're it!" and race in the opposite direction. This should entice her to stop and follow you. In all games of chase, always have your dog chase you—never chase your dog.

When teaching your dog the *come* command, you need to make sure that she does not associate the word "come" with any negativity. If your dog associates the *come* command with being on the receiving end of your anger for misbehaving, you need to create a new verbal cue and then be certain to use positive reinforcement every time your dog obeys this new command. Rather than

telling your dog to come, you might try “here,” “now,” or even “bye.” Whatever verbal cue you select, you must be consistent. Make sure other members of your household also convert to this new word.

Sitting Pretty with the *Sit* Command

Consider the *sit* command as integral to your dog's proficiency in matters of etiquette. People love being greeted by dogs, but no one really craves being knocked over by an exuberant Labrador retriever or splattered with muddy paw prints by an overenthusiastic Jack Russell terrier. To a dog, there's nothing wrong with greeting a fellow canine by jumping up on him. Therefore, it's up to you to train your dog to greet your two-legged friends properly.

Mastering the *sit* command will certainly win your canine lots of compliments, which becomes a bonus for you!

Okay, let's look at some ways to get your dog to sit on cue. The easiest method is simply to catch your dog in the act of sitting. The second he does so on his own, tell him he has performed a good sit. Praise him and give him a treat. (In fact, you should keep a few treats in your pocket so you can deliver the payoff each time he sits voluntarily.)

The first method in getting your dog to sit on cue is called Go with Gravity. Consider this a hands-free method of training your dog to sit. No one really enjoys being forced physically into a position. Your dog is no different. This method taps into the powers of gravity. With your dog in front of you—probably sporting a quizzical look

because he has no idea what you plan to do next—take your right hand and slowly glide it up and over his head. Use a lot of animation in your voice as you tell him to sit. Your bedazzled dog should be following your hand as you

SIT, GOOD SIT!

guide it up and over his head toward his tail. This is where gravity plays a vital role. No dog—no matter the breed—can arch his head back to follow your hand without his rump hitting the floor. The second it does, tell him good sit, and heap on the praise. Repeat four or five times per session. In time, your dog should be able to fall into a sitting position with your hand signal and without the need for any vocal cues.

The second method to getting your dog to sit is called The Nose Knows. Dogs are sniff masters—they have a nose for everything, from the scent of a rose to a chewed tennis ball hidden in thick groundcover. In fact, they can smell things more keenly—and at greater distances—than people can even dream of. Use your dog's super smelling ability to your advantage when reinforcing the *sit* command. Select a high-quality treat your dog absolutely craves. (A tip: Use this treat only when you are training him to do something. It makes the treat even more appealing.) Hold this treat at the tip of your dog's nose and move it slightly up and back toward your dog's hind end so that he must lift his head up and follow it. This is an effective luring method. It gets your dog to follow the treat with his nose and plop his rear end down. As soon as he does, ask for a sit and then give him the treat. Repeat four or five times per session and always end on a successful sit response.

Some dogs can't help themselves. They just have to chase down a flung object and bring it back to you. If this sounds like your dog then use this behavior trait to your advantage by using the method A Fetching Way to Sit. When you play a game of retrieve—whether your dog is bounding after a tennis ball, Frisbee, or other prized object—always incorporate the *sit* command as part of the fun.

Teach your fetch-happy canine that he must always bring back the object, drop it, and sit in front of you before you toss it again. And, again and again. Finally, give a cue to signal fetch time has ended, such as "game over." You can do this using a hand-sweeping motion similar to what a baseball umpire uses as a signal to indicate that a base runner is safe at home plate. You cross your hands in front of you and then open your arms wide. Then, immediately pick up the toy and leave the area. This teaches your dog that you are the wonderful keeper of the toys, the person who initiates and ends all games.

As a side bonus to this game, you never have to worry about your dog accidentally nipping your fingers when trying to wrestle the ball from you or getting into an unwanted game of keep-away with the ball in his mouth. Plus, it's a fun way to get him to sit.

Who said the *sit* command must be boring? Spice up lesson time with Canine Push-ups—this fun game is anything but boring. As a bonus, your dog gets to ham it up and may not even realize you are honing his proficiency responding to the *sit* command.

With your dog facing you, place a tasty treat in your right hand. Move it close to your dog's nose to let him sniff it. Do not let him nibble at it. Lure his head back for a sit. When he does, move the treat straight down in front of his paws. His head will follow. Then, with the treat at floor level, move it away from your dog's front paws to force him to lie down. Think of these two moves as doing an "L" with a treat. Then, quickly repeat these steps so it appears as if your dog is doing a series of canine-style push-ups. Ask him to sit down, quickly in a happy voice (not like a Marine drill instructor) and watch your dog have fun performing. Don't forget to hand over the treat after a few successful push-ups.

The Way to Stay

Your dog has mastered the *come* and the *sit* commands. Now comes the third essential command—*stay*. Dogs want to be by our sides. If they had their way, they would shadow at work, at home, and even on dates or trips to the dentist.

The *stay* command should be taught in baby steps, so you can build up trust and confidence in your canine and so she knows you don't plan on abandoning her.

Before you can begin the *stay* command lesson, your dog must consistently heed your *watch me* command, because

you need eye contact and complete attention from your dog when you issue the command to stay in one place. It is easy to teach your dog this command, especially when you have some delicious treats with you. First, address your dog by their name and tell her to watch you. Then, take a small piece of treat in your fingers and move it up toward the side of your eye. The goal is to get your dog's eyes to watch the treat move. As soon as your dog looks you in the eye, hand over the treat. Repeat a few times each day so that your dog will quickly learn that the *watch me* command reaps some tasty dividends for complying. With the *watch me* command under your belt, you can now learn to do the *stay* command.

Divide the *stay* command into time, distance, and distractions. Wait until your dog can stay on command for a few seconds close to you in a quiet area before you extend the time, distance, and distractions. Build on each success. With the *stay* command, you must also incorporate the ever-important *release* command, so your dog knows when it is okay to get up from that position. You can use a hand signal like raising your hand up with palms facing upward as you say "release," or "okay," or another word of your choosing. Just be consistent—always use the same word and hand signal to

release your dog from the sit position.

Dogs have a short attention span. Your mission with the *stay* command is to increase gradually the length of time you want your dog to remain in one place. Don't expect your dog to sit for more than a few seconds the first few times you tell her to stay.

Start with the basics by getting your dog in a down position. Wait a second or two before you tell her she has performed a good stay. At the same time, use your hand in a motion like a traffic cop signaling a stop to oncoming cars. Then, reward with a treat.

Purposely delay the reward to teach your dog you are requesting she stay put. With each *stay* command, gradually extend the time you reward a treat from two to five to 10 seconds and beyond. If your eager dog should get up and move before the designated time, do not give a treat. Initially, aim for a stay that lasts 30 seconds to a minute in a quiet, undistracted place in your home or backyard.

Once your dog consistently demonstrates she can stay put while you are an arm's reach away, you're ready to add the second key step in the *stay* command lesson—increasing the space between you and your dog. Start by getting your dog to stay for 30 seconds or so with you a foot or two away. Praise and reward. Then, take a few steps back and repeat the procedure. If your dog starts to get up, say "uh-uh" or other sound, look away, and do not treat. Ask your dog to sit and try again. Your goal is to walk across the room or backyard with your dog in a sitting or down position. Once you are across the room, tell your dog to release and then ask her to come as your dog gets up and bounds your way. Praise and treat.

Now that your dog has proven consistently that she can stay for up to a minute or more in your house or other place where you've controlled the environment it's time for the final step of the *stay* command lesson: getting your dog to comply when there are distractions. This is very important because your dog does not live in a bubble or in an environment that you can always control. Things happen—a stray cat suddenly appears on the sidewalk, or a skateboard whizzes by—and your dog wants to give chase.

That's where the *stay* command keeps her safely by your side.

Start with mild distractions, such as having a friend walk by as you tell your dog to stay. Then have this friend walk by with a dog who your dog likes. Have someone bang on a pot or pan as you give a lesson. Go slowly and encourage her. Most of all, be patient. Remember: Deliver

food treats and praise only when your dog ignores the increasingly tempting distractions.

The Step on That Leash method rewards your dog for doing basically nothing—just chilling. Put a leash on your dog and have her sit or get into a down position by your side as you watch television, work on your computer, or engage in some other sedentary activity. Without your dog knowing, stash a handful of treats near your hand—but out of her reach. When your dog stays put for 10 to 20 seconds, quietly bring a treat down to her nose and tell her she performed a good stay. If she leaps up for more, ignore her. Only reward

her when she is stationary for at least 10 seconds.

To help a rambunctious dog, subtly keep one of your feet on her leash so she cannot get up and move about. When she tries, she quickly realizes she can't move far. Wait until she lies down again for at least 10 seconds before you hand her a treat and praise her. Gradually increase the time between your praise and treats.

Let's Call It a Wrap

Congratulations! By following these tips, guides, and games, you've emerged as the benevolent leader in your dog's mind—the person he is eager to please. And, you've done it by being consistent and positive. In return, you will be able to share your life with a dog who is both compliant and happy. Who knows? In no time, your very obedient, smart dog may be demonstrating other skills, such as fetching your paper, sitting nicely under your table at an outdoor café, and maybe even doing your taxes!

Arden Moore is an award-winning author who specializes in writing about pets and on human health topics. Moore belongs to the Dog Writers Association of America and the Association of Veterinary Communicators. She has authored numerous books, including *Healthy Dog, Dog Training, Happy Dog*, and *Dog Parties*. She shares her home with her dog, Chipper, and three dog-like cats, Murphy, Little Guy, and Callie. She can be reached through her Web site: www.byarden.com.

Buck Jones's humorous illustrations have appeared in numerous magazines (including *Dog Fancy* and *Cat Fancy*) and books. He is the illustrator for the best-selling Simple Solutions series books, *Why Do Cockatiels Do That?, Why Do Parakeets Do That?, Kittens! Why Do They Do What They Do?*, and *Puppies! Why Do They Do What They Do?*.